30p

WITHDRAWN FROM STOCK

16 AUG 1996

EARL SHILTON LIBRARY
TEL: 42467

Libraries & Information

19 MAR 1988   12. FEB. 1990   -15. FEB. 1992   13 SEP
                23. FEB. 1990   01. OCT
. 10. NOV. 1988   27. AUG. 19
  -9. FEB. 1989 15. JUN. 1990   07. NOV
  -3. MAR. 1989 9 JULY 1990   08. MAY 07. NOV
                 30. MAY 1991   24. AUG
  19. MAY 1989 -5. OCT. 1991   13. FEB 95
  28. JUL. 1989   10. AUG

Our World

JUNGLES AND RAINFORESTS

Theodore Rowland-Entwistle

Titles in this series

Coasts	Polar Regions
Deserts	Rivers and Lakes
Grasslands	Seas and Oceans
Jungles and Rainforests	Temperate Forests
Mountains	The Earth in Space

First published in 1987 by
Wayland (Publishers) Ltd
61 Western Road, Hove
East Sussex BN3 1JD. England

© Copyright 1987 Wayland (Publishers) Ltd

Edited by Susan Bullen
Designed by Malcolm Smythe

British Library Cataloguing in Publication Data:
Rowland-Entwistle, Theodore
  Jungles and rainforests.—(Our world)
  1. Jungle ecology—Juvenile literature
  I. Title II. Series
  574.5'2642'0913 QH541.5.J8
  ISBN 0–85078–874–9

Typeset by DP Press, Sevenoaks, Kent
Printed in Italy by G. Canale & C.s.p.A., Turin.
Bound in Belgium by Casterman S.A.

Front cover main photograph A canopy of leaves and epiphytes in the tropical rainforest of Queensland, Australia.

Front cover inset photograph A colourful South American macaw.

Back cover A Pygmy man in the African rainforest carrying an elephant spear.

Contents

Chapter 1 Introducing rainforests

What are rainforests?	4
Classifying rainforests	6
Where are the rainforests?	8

Chapter 2 Life in the rainforests

The struggle for light	10
Flowers and fruit	12
Life in the canopy	14
Life on the ground	16

Chapter 3 Rainforest variations

Differences in plants	18
Differences in trees	20
Differences in mammals and birds	22
Differences in insects	24

Chapter 4 People and rainforests

Rainforest peoples	26
Exploring the forests	28
Farming in rainforests	30

Chapter 5 Rainforest resources

Timber	32
Other rainforest products	34

Chapter 6 Rainforests in danger

The importance of rainforests	36
The disappearing rainforests	38
The threat to wildlife and people	40
Saving the rainforests	42

Glossary	44
Further reading	45
Index	46

CHAPTER 1 INTRODUCING RAINFORESTS

What are rainforests?

Rainforests are so called because they grow in those parts of the world where there is heavy rain all the year round. They flourish in or near the tropics, the hot regions that lie either side of the equator. The atmosphere in a tropical rainforest is permanently humid – hot and damp.

A rainforest is often referred to as a jungle, which is a Hindi word from India meaning a wilderness. A true jungle is a thick tangle of vegetation, through which people have to force and cut their way. Rainforests contain patches of jungle, but mainly they are more open. The forest floor is covered with rotting leaves.

Rainforest trees are very tall broadleaved evergreens. The tallest trees have buttress roots, wing-like growths that spread out from the base of the trunk to act as props, while others have stilt roots which grow down from the trunk or branches, often in graceful arches. All the trees carry their branches and leaves at the top of long slender trunks, forming a huge umbrella-like green canopy. The dense canopy filters much of the daylight, leaving a shady green world beneath it.

The rainforests contain more different species (kinds) of plants and animals than any other part of the world – even more than the oceans that cover nearly three-quarters of the earth. A forest in the tropics has between five and twenty times as many species of trees as one in the temperate zone of North America or Europe, but there are relatively few of each species. Rainforests provide a home for many of the world's most fascinating animals.

The rainforests are a vast storehouse of substances potentially useful to humans. We already owe many of our foods and medicines to them, as well as much of our timber. Sadly, having survived virtually unchanged for millions of years, these precious rainforests are now being destroyed at an alarming rate.

Right Dense rainforest flourishes around the Amazon.

4

Classifying rainforests

Not all rainforests are alike. They vary according to local conditions, such as the prevailing winds, their height above sea level, the amount of rain that falls and how far they are from the equator, the hottest region of the earth.

At the equator day and night are of equal length. This does not mean that there are twelve hours of uninterrupted sunshine because the sky is often cloudy and rain, when it comes, falls in torrents. A tropical storm can produce as much as 20 cm (8 inches) of rain in an hour.

The world's rainforests may be divided into six kinds: tropical; montane (mountain); upper montane or cloud; monsoon; mangrove; and subtropical.

Tropical rainforests grow in moist lowland areas of the tropical region, such as the Amazon valley. These lush forests are the richest in plant and animal life.

Montane rainforests grow on mountain slopes in tropical areas. The higher they are above sea level, the less luxuriant they are because the climate is cooler.

Cloud forests grow at or above the normal cloud level on mountains. They are swathed in mist for most of the time.

A lush tropical rainforest of South America with ferns, bamboos and epiphytes on the trees.

Mist hangs over the trees of this South American cloud forest.

Monsoon forests grow in Southeast Asia. The monsoon is a seasonal wind. From October to March it blows from the north-east, and produces dry weather. From April to September it blows from the south-west, bringing rain.

Mangrove forests grow in swampy land near tropical or subtropical coasts. The dominant trees are mangroves, which flourish when their roots are regularly flooded by brackish (slightly salty) tidal water.

Subtropical rainforests lie just outside the tropics, for example in southern China and eastern Australia.

The two diagrams below show the seasonal pattern of the monsoon. From April to September the south-west monsoon blows across the Indian Ocean to India, where it deposits the moisture it picked up from the sea, bringing the rainy season. The south-east monsoon brings rain to Southeast Asia and Australia. From October to March the north-east monsoon blows from central Asia across India, bringing the dry season. Pictured below are monsoon rain clouds gathering over the monsoon forest of Sri Lanka.

South-west Monsoon

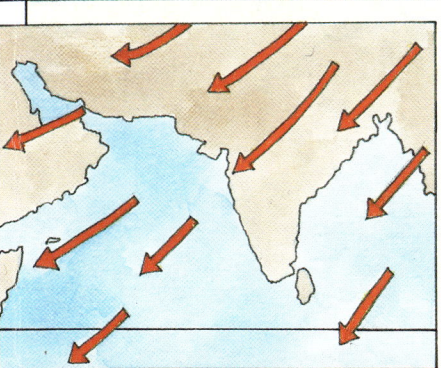
North-east Monsoon

7

Where are the rainforests?

Rainforests lie in three main regions in the tropical zone either side of the equator, wherever the climate is hot and wet. Over half (57 per cent) of the tropical rainforests are in South and Central America, a quarter are in Southeast Asia, and the rest are in Africa. More than thirty countries have some rainforest within their borders. Brazil has the biggest share, with a third of the world's rainforests.

The South American rainforest lies largely in the basin of the Amazon River. It extends westwards to the Andes Mountains, east and north into the Guianas, and south to the edge of the Gran Chaco, the vast plain that lies west of the Paraná and Paraguay rivers.

Besides this huge continuous area, there are smaller strips of rainforest to the west of the Andes, in Colombia and Ecuador, and along the eastern coast of Brazil. There is a further belt of rainforest along the eastern coast of South America, and more as far north as southern Mexico. Some of the West Indian islands also contain rainforest.

The Southeast Asian rainforest extends from Burma south to Thailand and the Malay Peninsula, and through the islands of Indonesia and the Philippines. From New Guinea it continues as a narrow strip in north-eastern Australia. Some Pacific islands also have patches of rainforest.

The largest part of the African rainforest lies in the basin of the Zaïre River. It extends westwards along the coast as far as Guinea, broken by a strip of dry land in Ghana, Togo, Benin and Nigeria. Patches of forest exist in eastern Africa, and there is a narrow strip along the eastern coast of Madagascar.

Subtropical rainforests occur in southern China, eastern Australia, northern New Zealand and South Korea.

As a result of logging and forest clearance in South America, Africa and Southeast Asia, the world has already lost vast amounts of rainforest.

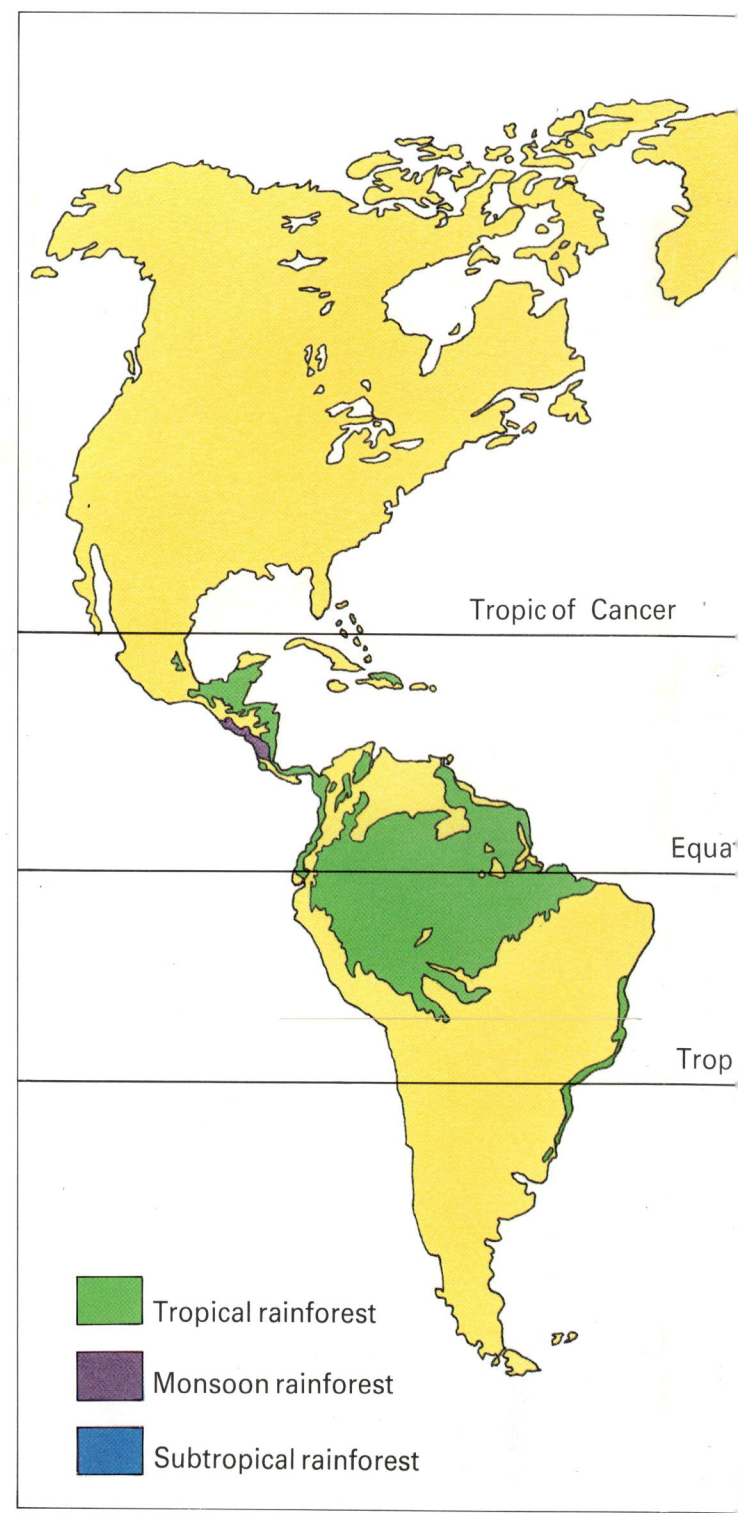

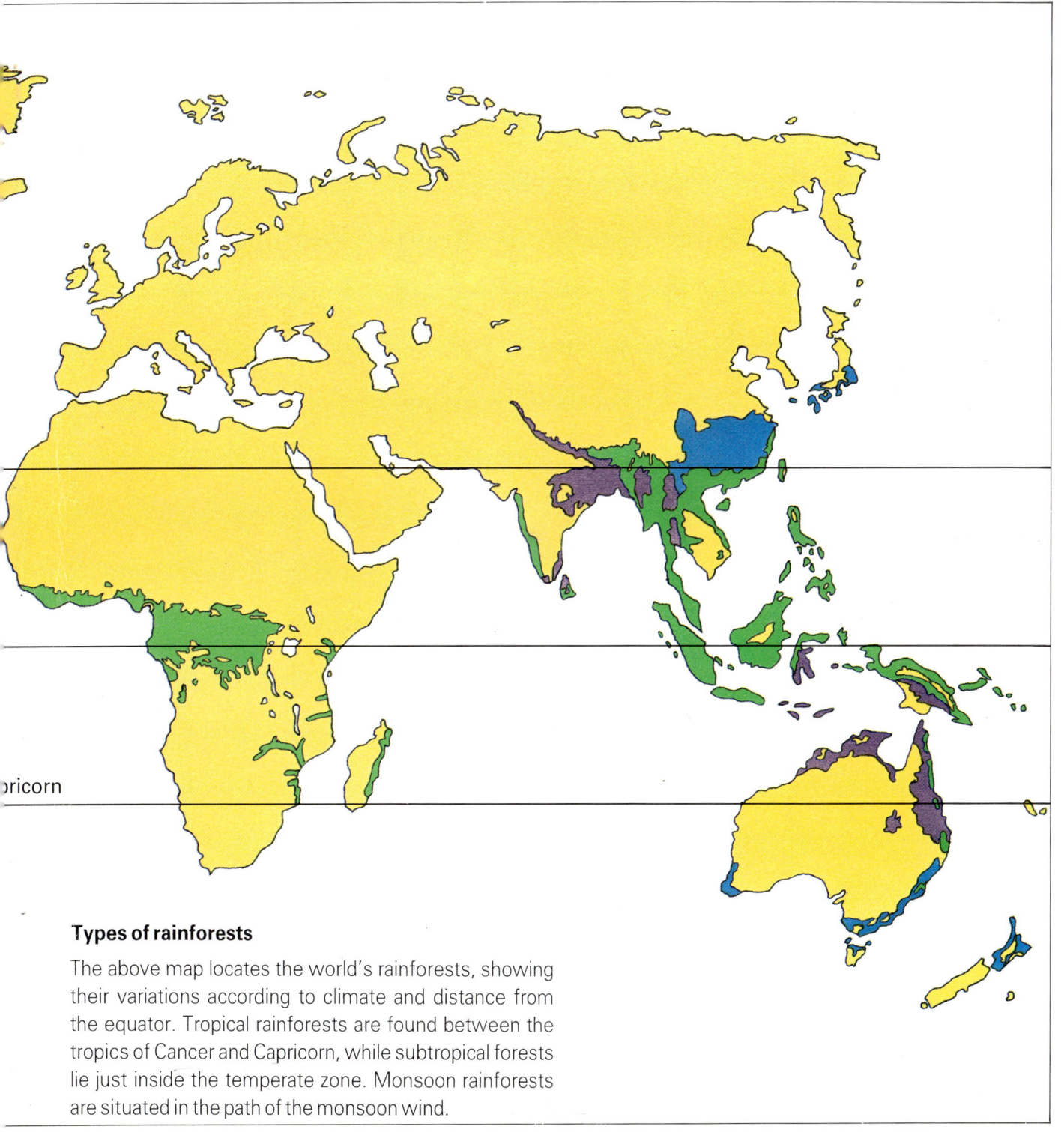

Types of rainforests

The above map locates the world's rainforests, showing their variations according to climate and distance from the equator. Tropical rainforests are found between the tropics of Cancer and Capricorn, while subtropical forests lie just inside the temperate zone. Monsoon rainforests are situated in the path of the monsoon wind.

CHAPTER 2 LIFE IN THE RAINFORESTS

The struggle for light

Most of the plants in a tropical rainforest are tall evergreen trees. Generally speaking, they shed their leaves a few at a time throughout the year, so the forest is always green. The trees are engaged in a struggle to reach the light. Like many other plants, they carry their leaves at such angles that the tree avoids shading itself as far as possible. Their branches and leaves grow at the top of very tall, bare trunks, forming a green canopy. This main layer is between 30 and 45 metres (100–150 ft) above the ground. A few trees up to 60 metres (200 ft) in height rise above the canopy in what is called the emergent layer.

The canopy casts so much shade that only one-hundredth of the light falling on the forest reaches the ground below. A group of trees less than 10 metres (33 ft) tall forms what is called the understorey. They are mostly young trees whose growth is stunted by lack of light. The young trees get their chance when one of the giants above them comes crashing down, its life ended, and lets the light stream through. For a while plant life at ground level can flourish, creating a real patch of jungle. Elsewhere in the green dimness there are only mosses, liverworts and a few herbs that do not need much light. A huge variety of saprophytic

A thick tangle of lianas strangle one other in their search for light, leaving darkness beneath them.

plants, such as fungi, flourish in the dark, moist forest, feeding on dead wood and leaf litter on the forest floor. Rainforest fungi are extremely varied in shape and size, and some are even luminous.

Interesting plants of jungles and rainforests are lianas. These are woody vines which, like ivy in the cool woodlands of the north, make their way towards the light by climbing up the trunks of trees. They cling on by means of tendrils or hooks and may even send out small roots to burrow into the tree bark. When they reach the light they produce their flowers. Some lianas are quite fine, while others are thick and as strong as ropes.

Vegetation layers of the rainforest

The diagram on the left illustrates the layers of vegetation found in a tropical rainforest. The forest floor is composed of leaf litter, fungi and, where sufficient light filters through the trees, low herbs and ferns. The next layer consists of taller shrubs and small trees, and is known as the understorey. There is often a large gap between the understorey and the lowest branches of the main group of trees, which form the canopy. These trees reach a height of about 30 m (100 ft) and from above the dense mass of tree crowns resembles a field of cabbages. Rising above the crowns of the canopy layer are a few giant trees which form the emergent layer.

Decomposition

The rainforest floor is a thin layer of decaying leaves and animal remains which are broken down into humus by bacteria and insects. The humus is eaten by small insects and is absorbed into the roots of the trees.

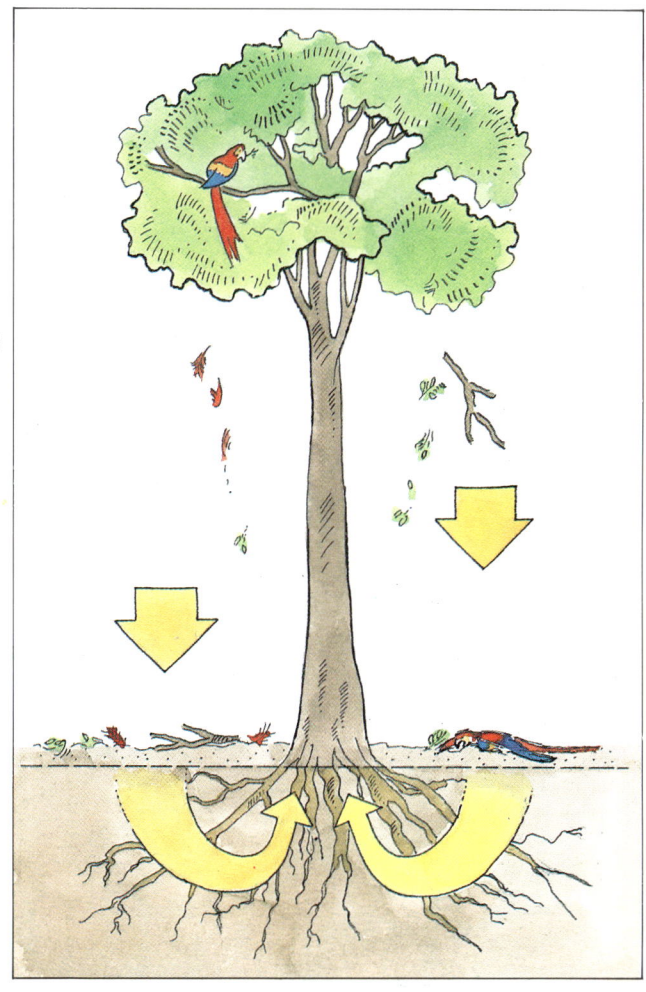

Flowers and fruit

Because temperature and rainfall in a tropical rainforest are constant all the year round, there are no flowering and fruiting seasons. At any time of year, some plants are in flower and others are bearing fruit.

At ground level the occasional patch of colour is provided by flowering plants which require little light. However, the more colourful flowers are mostly found higher up in the canopy. Most of the tall trees, especially those in the emergent layer, can be pollinated by wind and so have rather inconspicuous flowers. In the sheltered canopy the fruit trees bear scented, more colourful flowers to attract birds, insects and animals to pollinate them. Many fruits of rainforest trees hang on long stalks. Varieties include banana, mango, guava, passion fruit, papaya and breadfruit.

Most of the colour in rainforests is provided by epiphytic plants. These grow high up on the trunks, branches and even the leaves of giant trees of the

The delicate spray of an epiphytic orchid growing on a thick branch of a rainforest tree.

Not all fruit bats feed on fruit. Shown left is a long-tongued fruit bat of Southeast Asia feeding on a tropical rainforest flower. As it feeds, pollen grains stick on to the bat. When the bat moves on to feed on another flower, it deposits the pollen grains from the last flower, so pollinating it and helping it to produce fruit. Bats which feed on fruit help fruit trees to reproduce. The bat's droppings contain seeds from the fruit it has eaten. In time, the seeds contained in the droppings on the forest floor will become new trees bearing flowers and fruit, so completing the cycle.

Clusters of bananas surround the long stalk, bearing the banana flower.

canopy. Most epiphytes do not draw food from their host trees, but absorb moisture from the air with their aerial roots. By growing high up, these plants receive enough light to produce flowers. Of all the epiphytes, the orchids are the most spectacular. They have blooms of all colours, blue being the rarest, and produce an immense variety of shapes to attract insects to pollinate them.

The climbing vines of jungles and rainforests also produce many attractive flowers, such as various kinds of passion flower, the trumpet-like *ipomoeas* (brilliantly coloured types of convolvulus) and the bell-shaped *Cobaea scandens*, all of South America.

Bright flowers are particularly attractive to the beautiful tropical butterflies and to some birds. The tiny, but brightly coloured South American hummingbirds penetrate the blooms with their long bills, pollinating the flowers as they drink the nectar from them.

A flamboyant red passion flower of the Amazon rainforest.

Life in the canopy

Animal life in a tropical rainforest goes on at more than one level. A few animals live on or near the ground. The majority, however, including the most colourful, make their home high up in the airy, sunny world of the canopy, where there are plenty of leaves and fruit to eat.

High up in the canopy, vividly coloured butterflies flit from flower to flower. Below the treetops, monkeys howl and scream as they swing from branch to branch in search of fruit. By contrast, the fruit bats of Africa and Southeast Asia are silent. These bats hunt by day and by sight, unlike their blind night-flying relatives, which are guided by sound waves. They are generally larger than the night-fliers. The biggest, the flying fox, has a wingspan of 2 m (6 ft).

Hundreds of birds with colourful plumage live lower down in the canopy. The noisiest and gaudiest are the parrots that live in the South American rainforest. One of the largest and brightest is the red and green macaw, but there are fourteen other species of macaw that are nearly as colourful. The African grey parrot, which has a bright red tail, is common in African rainforests. The most striking of the parrots of Southeast Asia and Australasia is the great black cockatoo of New Guinea, which can crack the hardest nuts with its hooked beak.

A quiet animal of the canopy is the sloth of the Amazon area, which hangs upside down in the trees. Sloths move very slowly and rest for nineteen hours out of the twenty-four. Other tree dwellers include squirrels, rats and mice. In Australia a number of marsupials such as the phalangers (called possums by Australians) live in the treetops. In the forests of New Guinea and Queensland tree kangaroos leap from tree to tree, gripping branches with their long claws.

Brightly-coloured tree frogs live in the lower branches, as do reptiles like snakes and lizards. Millions of insects live in the canopy, either on the trees or as parasites on canopy animals.

A baby three-toed sloth clings on to its mother in the rainforest of Panama.

The aptly-named flying fox is an elegant member of the family of fruit bats.

Canopy dwellers of the South American rainforest

Life on the ground

The forest floor is home for a group of animals known as decomposers because they help to speed up the process of rotting down dead plant and animal matter that has fallen from the canopy. Decomposers include fungi, bacteria, worms, ants, termites, beetles, cockroaches, millipedes, and minute soil-dwelling insects. They are so numerous that most of the decaying plant and animal matter is very rapidly broken down.

Scavengers, such as vultures, make their way into the dim green corners of the forest, where they feed on the carcases of animals that have fallen from the canopy, such as monkeys and sloths.

Life is much more varied and lively in the jungle areas that grow up around the edges of the forests, such as on river banks, or in the clearings that form when a giant tree crashes to the ground, perhaps taking other smaller trees with it.

Tapirs are large, hoofed animals with a trunk-like snout that live in South American and Southeast Asian rainforests. They forage for food amongst the undergrowth and are excellent swimmers. In Southeast Asian forests the mouse deer can be found, while the tiny royal antelope lives in some African forests, both feeding on fallen nuts, fruits and leaves. Though elephants are generally found in the open grasslands, some live in forest margins of Africa and Asia.

A number of small members of the cat family, such as the jungle cat of Asia and the ocelot of South America live and hunt in the forests. Of the larger cats, the jaguar of South America and the leopard of Africa and Asia are the best-known, their spotted coats providing good camouflage in the dappled light under the trees. In Indian and Southeast Asian rainforests, tigers roam wild.

Various large birds dwell on the forest floor, such as the jungle fowl in Malaysia, bright pheasants of Southeast Asia, and the cock-of-the-rock of South America. The males of this species perform an elaborate dance when courting the females.

A tiny blunt-headed tree snake slithers down a *Heliconia* plant growing on the forest floor in Ecuador.

The Brazilian tapir, *Tapirus terrestris*, is the most widespread of the South American tapirs.

A leopard stalking in the Sri Lankan rainforest.

CHAPTER 3 RAINFOREST VARIATIONS

Differences in plants

Although rainforests all occur within the tropical region, the plant life in them varies considerably. To see how this has come about we must go back 200 million years – a long time, but short in the history of the earth.

At that time all the continents as we know them today were joined together in one landmass, which scientists refer to as Pangaea. About 180 million years ago Pangaea started to break up, first into two supercontinents, Gondwanaland and Laurasia, and then into the present day continents. These continents have drifted to their familiar positions at a rate of around 25 mm (1 inch) a year, and are still moving.

In Pangaea, Africa was joined to South America on one side, and to India, Antarctica and Australia on the other. Plant life may well have been very similar throughout this huge landmass, but after the continents separated, their plants evolved independently to produce the great diversity of species we have today.

As the continents moved, so their climates changed. Scientists believe this may explain not only the difference in the species of plants between one continent and another, but also the great contrast in the numbers of different species.

The rainforest of Southeast Asia covers a smaller area than that of either Africa or South America, but has probably the richest plant life. Each part of its forests contains a great many different species. The island of Borneo alone has at least 10,000 species. Africa has much the fewest number of species of trees and plants, and in general its forests are less varied than those of South America and, especially, Southeast Asia.

One group of epiphytes is found only in South

When the continents were joined together in Pangaea (diagram 1), it is likely that the plant life of the rainforests was quite similar because general conditions in this huge landmass were fairly uniform. As the continents broke up into their present positions (diagram 2), plant life evolved differently in each one.

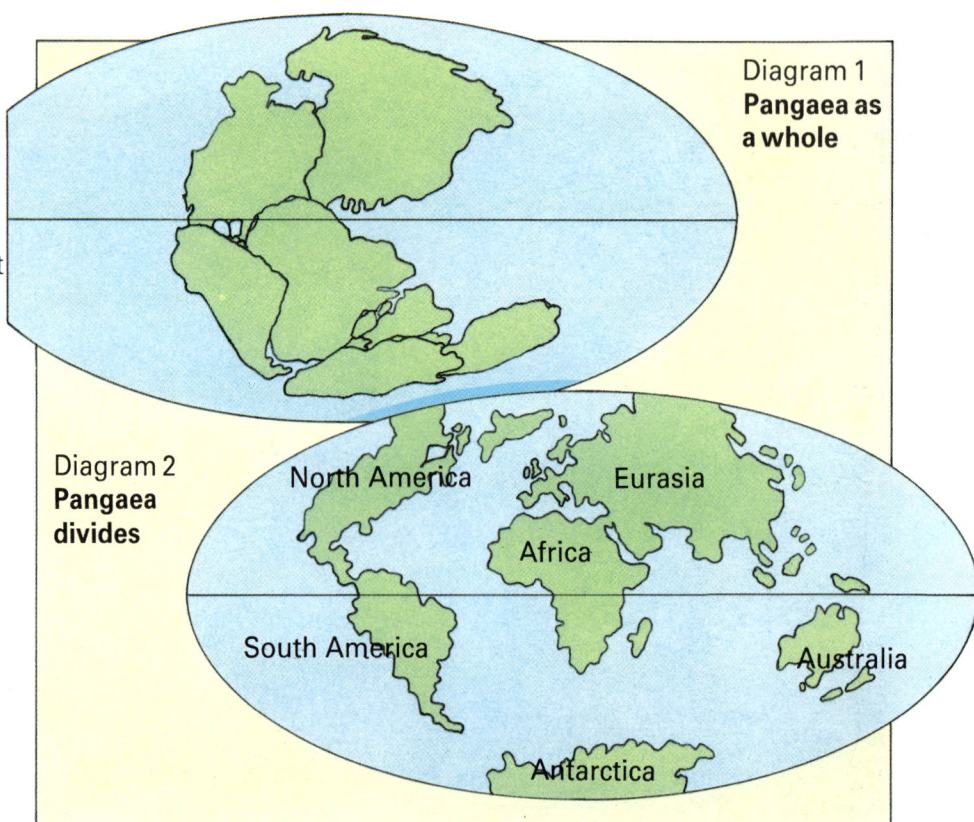

Diagram 1
Pangaea as a whole

Diagram 2
Pangaea divides

18

The striking flower of a bromeliad in Ecuador.

America. The plants are called bromeliads and are related to pineapples. Their waxy leaves form large rosettes which act as tanks, catching water and debris falling from the canopy above. The largest of these tanks may hold as much as 55 litres (12 gallons), forming small ponds in which many insects and small tree frogs live.

In parts of the Amazon rainforest, the giant waterlily, *Victoria amazonica*, grows in shallow lagoons. Its vast saucer-shaped leaves, covered in spiny prickles, can grow to 2 m (7 ft) in diameter.

However, the Indonesian island of Sumatra must boast the strangest flower of all. The plant *Rafflesia* is parasitic upon the roots of rainforest trees and produces a deep red, leathery flower measuring a metre (3 ft) in width. Another feature of the flower is the strong smell of rotting flesh which it gives off. The smell attracts flies which pollinate the flower.

The peculiar and enormous flower of *Rafflesia*, growing in Sumatra.

19

Differences in trees

Rainforests vary in type according to what part of the world they are in, the climate of the region, and its height above sea level. These conditions affect the species of trees, which grow best in a particular habitat, and the rate at which they grow.

For example, the monsoon rainforests of Southeast Asia have two distinct seasons, wet and dry. The trees there have adapted to these changes. During the dry season the tall deciduous trees in the canopy shed their leaves, in order to avoid losing too much moisture through them by transpiration. While the tall trees are bare, the smaller trees and shrubs below grow rapidly because they receive more sunlight. When the wet season starts, the taller trees burst into leaf, flourishing on the increased moisture.

Mangrove forests grow in very different conditions – humid swampy areas near coasts or in river estuaries, in tropical or subtropical regions. Mangrove trees are evergreens which need salty water around their roots. The trees send down long extra roots from their branches, until an individual tree may have hundreds of roots, and the resulting mangrove thicket looks like a forest on stilts. The thick tangle of roots traps silt, and gradually builds up the land. Some mangroves produce conical air roots which grow upwards out of the mud, bringing air to the tree.

The mangroves provide a home in their canopy for birds and monkeys, while many different crabs and the amphibious fish called mudskippers live in the mud around their roots.

Cloud forests occur in mountainous tropical areas, where the heavy rainfall and the cooler conditions combine to keep the trees permanently shrouded in mist. Thinner soil and exposure to strong winds result in trees that do not grow as tall as those in the hot, humid lowlands. Ferns and mosses grow in abundance, flourishing in the moist conditions.

Weather-beaten, stunted trees of montane rainforest in Brazil.

Shown above is a thick tangle of mangrove roots growing near the Indian Ocean in East Africa. The typically arched, prop-like roots are barely anchored into the thick mud, so that vital air can be absorbed by surface roots. The young mangrove stalks have sprouted from seeds with long roots, which fall from the trees and take root in the mud.

Pictured below is an area of mangrove on the tropical south-western coast of India. To survive the regular flooding of sea water and mud, this type of mangrove produces conical aerial roots which grow upwards instead of downwards. Thus they can project above the water or mud and absorb air.

Differences in mammals and birds

The differences in the animal life of the various rainforests are even more striking than those of the plants. This is especially true of the mammals of Australia and New Guinea compared with those of the rest of the world. The only original Australian mammals – before settlers imported others – were marsupials (pouched animals whose young are born only partly developed) and two species of monotremes (egg-laying mammals) – the duck-billed platypus and the echidna.

These primitive mammals were able to survive in the isolation of Australia and New Guinea after they had become extinct elsewhere. In 1856 the British naturalist, Alfred Russel Wallace drew a line on the map – now known as Wallace's Line – which marks the boundary between the mammals of the rest of the world and those of Australia and New Guinea. It coincides with the ancient boundary between Gondwanaland and Laurasia. A few marsupials, such as opposums, have survived in South America, which was also isolated for millions of years. The South American rainforest is noted for its lack of large mammals. The largest is the

One of the brightest of South American birds must surely be the red-necked tanager.

Old World and New World monkeys
Old World monkeys of Africa and Asia do not have a prehensile tail, their cheeks and forehead tend to be hairy, and their noses have close-set nostrils. In contrast, New World monkeys of South America often have prehensile tails, bare faces and flatter noses. Shown above are two Old World monkeys – the mandrill, with its brightly coloured face and stumpy tail, and the colobus monkey, a superb acrobat with a non-prehensile tail. The straight tail helps the colobus monkey to balance as it leaps from tree to tree. Also shown are two New World monkeys – the small, delicate squirrel monkey with its slightly prehensile tail, and the long-limbed acrobatic spider monkey with its fully prehensile tail, which it uses as an extra limb.

tapir, which is about 100 cm (40 in) high.

There are marked differences between rainforest monkeys. Those of South America have bare faces with flattened noses and prehensile (grasping) tails, while those of Africa and Southeast Asia have less flat noses and non-prehensile tails.

Lemurs are mostly nocturnal animals restricted to Madagascar, while related lorises are found in the rainforests of India and Southeast Asia.

South America has been called 'the bird continent' with toucans, tanagers, quetzals and over 160 species of hummingbird in its rainforests.

In Africa long-billed sunbirds also feed on nectar, just like the hummingbirds. A most interesting African bird is the indicator bird, or honeyguide. It feeds on wax from wild bees' nests. It obtains this by persuading the honey badger, or ratel, to open the nest and eat the honey, leaving the wax for the bird to eat.

The forests of Australia and New Guinea have three unique bird groups – the bowerbirds, the colourful birds of paradise, and the flightless cassowaries.

Red tree kangaroos, a rare sight in the tropical rainforest of north-east Australia.

The slender loris of India and Southeast Asia is a slow, nocturnal creature.

Differences in insects

The rainforests are positively alive with insects. Zoologists have identified more than a million species but they suspect that there may be twenty times as many still to be discovered and listed. Like the plants, insects in the tropical forests include many extra large kinds. Among them are the goliath beetle of Africa which is more than 14 cm (5½ inches) long; the American robber-fly, with a wingspan of nearly 6.5 cm (2½ inches); and huge butterflies such as the giant swallowtail of Africa (wingspan 25 cm; 10 inches) and the vivid blue morpho butterfly of the Amazon region (wingspan 18 cm; 7 inches).

A large number of the flying insects live high in the canopy. Some make their home in the fur of larger animals – a sloth may have as many as 300 assorted moths, beetles, ticks and other small creatures living in its coat.

The most interesting of the ground dwellers are the ants and termites. Some species of ants make their homes on acacia trees, feeding on the trees' nectar. The ants most dreaded by other forest creatures are the army ants of South America. These creatures travel through the forest in armies of up to 20,000,000, making camp for a time and then marching forward again, eating everything in their path.

A curious sight on the rainforest floor is what appears to be moving leaves. In fact, on closer inspection, the leaves are being carried by leaf-cutter ants. They cut large pieces of leaf and carry them to their nest, where they chew the leaves to form a mulch. A special fungus grows on the mulch, on which the ants feed.

Rainforest termites construct elaborate soil nests with broad, conical roofs to keep the rain off. A tall nest with many roofs looks like a miniature Chinese pagoda.

Stick and leaf insects, as well as the praying mantis, are perfectly camouflaged, so that their predators will have difficulty seeing them amongst the leafy jungle.

Leaf cutter ants on their nest of leaves in the Brazilian rainforest.

This huge African goliath beetle is not much smaller than the banana it is eating.

The shimmering blue giant morpho butterfly of South America.

CHAPTER 4 PEOPLE AND RAINFORESTS

Rainforest peoples

To people from other parts of the world, the jungles and rainforests may seem wild, hostile places. But people have lived in them for thousands of years, and about a thousand tribes still do. These forest dwellers have learned how to use the plants of the forests, especially for medicine, and scientists in the industrialized countries are just starting to appreciate their traditional knowledge.

Hundreds of tribes of American Indians (Amerindians) used to live in the tropical forests of South America. Some of the Indians lived by hunting and gathering seeds. Others cleared land and farmed it. Their main food crop was cassava, from which tapioca is made. They also grew beans, maize and sweet potatoes.

Even today there are a few American Indian tribes living in the Amazonian rainforest. Some tribes still have no contact with the rest of the world. However, more than eighty tribes have died out since 1900.

In the African rainforests the original people were the Pygmies and the Bushmen, who average less than 1.5 m (5 ft) tall. Their ways of life were similar to those of the American Indian forest dwellers, though they grew different crops. A Pygmy tribe, the Mbuti, still live in the forests of Zaïre. The remaining Bushmen now roam the Kalahari Desert. Some of the taller Bantu-speaking people also live in the tropical forests. They spread from West Africa about 2,000 years ago and are now the dominant group south of the Sahara.

Pygmy peoples are also found in rainforests in

Typical Pygmy home

Rainforest dwellers make good use of forest materials when building their homes. The Pygmies of central Africa make their cone-shaped homes out of leaves and branches. First they make a framework of long, supple sticks which are tied together at the top in the centre. Then they tie branches widthwise across the frame, to strengthen it. Finally, the whole surface is covered with large leaves. Usually the women and children build such homes, which can be finished within one hour. A typical Pygmy home is shown on the left. The Amazon Indians of South America often build their homes on the banks of rivers, which are important for transport and fishing. The homes are made of wood with a sloping thatched roof. Some homes are built on stilts above the water. Shown on the right is a typical Amazon Indian home.

Members of a Daya tribe, who are hunters in the jungle of Borneo, Indonesia.

parts of Southeast Asia, for example in the Philippines. There are many other forest dwellers in Southeast Asia. In the wild, hilly lands of New Guinea there are about 700 tribes. Some, such as the Biami and the Gibusi, have ways of life that are similar to those of Stone Age people in Europe in prehistoric times. These people live in clearings in the forest, hunting and growing crops. As recently as 1970 some New Guinea tribes were reported to be cannibals.

In Borneo some people, such as the Sianh Daya in the central part of the island, live in villages in cleared areas. They depend for much of their living on the nearby jungle, where they not only hunt for food but also collect materials such as rattan, a climbing plant they use for basket-making.

Typical Amerindian home

27

Exploring the forests

Areas of Central and South America explored by Humboldt

The map above shows the areas of Central and South America explored by Baron von Humboldt. In 1800 he explored the regions of the rivers Amazon and Orinoco, studying the fascinating creatures and plants he discovered in the rainforest. He then explored high mountains of the Andes in Colombia and Peru, contributing greatly to the fields of geology and geography.

The first people to explore the rainforests were those who lived in and near them, such as the Amerindians, who first settled in the Amazonian region about 10,000 years ago.

Exploration by Europeans began with Christopher Columbus in 1492. In the journal of his first voyage to the Americas, he wrote the earliest description of a tropical rainforest: 'Trees of a thousand kinds and tall, and they seem to touch the sky, and some were flowering and some bearing fruit.'

The exploration of the American rainforests was continued by the *conquistadores* (conquerors), the hardy and ruthless handful of Spanish adventurers who overran the area now known as Latin America. Among them were Gonzalo Pizarro, governor of Quito in Peru, and his second-in-command Francisco de Orellana. They struck eastwards from the Andes mountains and fought their way for months through the rainforest until they came to the banks of the Napo River, a tributary of the Amazon.

While sailing down the Amazon, Orellana encountered a warlike group of Amerindian women, who reminded him of the Amazons of Greek legend – and so the river got its name.

The exploration of the African rainforest by Europeans began in the 1800s when many of the countries of Europe became interested in building empires in the continent. Among the explorers were Mungo Park, a Scottish surgeon who explored the Niger River region; the Scottish medical missionary David Livingstone, who explored southern and eastern Africa, seeking to bring an end to slavery; and the Welsh-American journalist Henry Morton Stanley, who travelled down the Zaïre River.

Scientific exploration of the rainforests was started in 1799 by the German geologist Baron von Humboldt, who made expeditions to South and Central America.

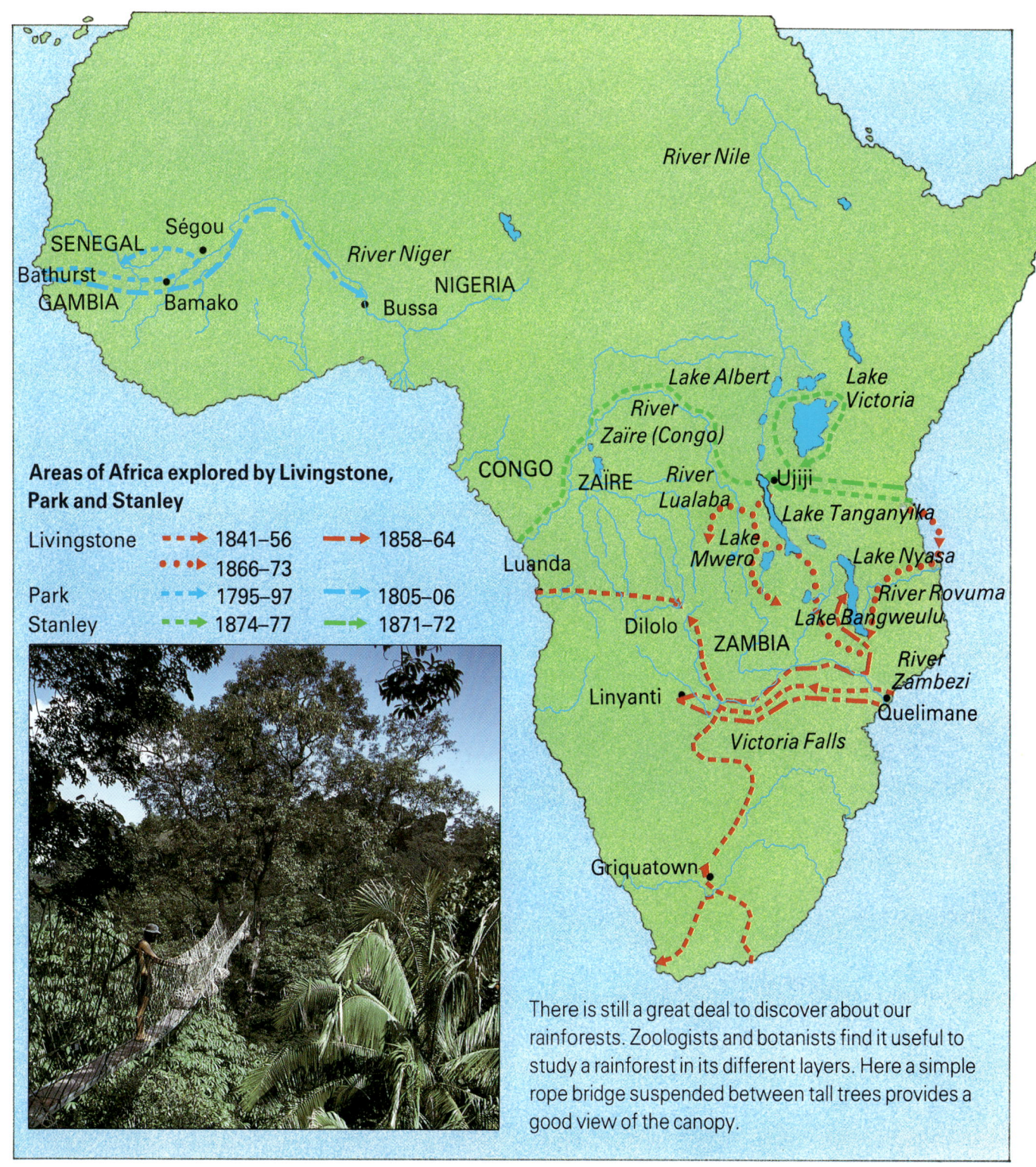

Areas of Africa explored by Livingstone, Park and Stanley

Livingstone ---> 1841–56   ---> 1858–64
            ····> 1866–73
Park   ---> 1795–97   ---> 1805–06
Stanley   ---> 1874–77   ---> 1871–72

There is still a great deal to discover about our rainforests. Zoologists and botanists find it useful to study a rainforest in its different layers. Here a simple rope bridge suspended between tall trees provides a good view of the canopy.

29

Farming in rainforests

The population of the Third World countries where the rainforests are located is increasing rapidly. Africa's population, about 530 million in 1986, is rising at about 3 per cent a year – which means it will double within 24 years. That of South America is rising at an annual rate of 2.4 per cent, while among those Southeast Asian countries with rainforests the population in Malaysia is rising by 3.2 per cent, and that of the Philippines is increasing by 2.7 per cent.

These increases create a demand for more food, and therefore more land on which to grow it. There is also a demand for food as a cash crop for sale to more prosperous countries. For example, nearly two-thirds of the rainforest in Central America has been cleared since 1950 to create grazing land for beef cattle. The United States buys 75 per cent of the beef produced.

The most basic form of rainforest farming is known as shifting cultivation. The people clear an area by the slash-and-burn method – felling the trees and burning the material cut down. Ash from the burning helps to fertilize the soil and a few good crops can be grown on it. But without further manuring or fertilization, or lying fallow (resting) for a year, rainforest soil quickly becomes exhausted. So the farmers abandon the site to the rapidly encroaching jungle and clear a fresh patch.

Shifting cultivation works reasonably well when only small numbers of people are involved. If there

Rainforest gives way to open fields and a plantation, Sri Lanka.

Picking cocoa pods in a banana and cocoa plantation in the tropical rainforest of Trinidad in the Caribbean.

are too many people, however, they have to reclear old sites that have not had time to recover from intensive farming, and so the crop yield is poor. Permanent settlement has much the same effect and is taking place on an ever-increasing scale, as modern technology opens up new roads through dense forest land and enables people to move there. For example, many thousands of new settlers have moved into the Rondônia region of the Brazilian rainforest, hoping to establish farms in newly-cleared areas. Many farmers, however, have not been successful and there have been violent conflicts between the vulnerable native peoples and the new landowners, whose life style is very different from that of the Amerindians.

Below Rainforests produce a wide variety of fruit and vegetables.

CHAPTER 5 RAINFOREST RESOURCES

Timber

Although farming is making serious inroads into the remaining tropical rainforests, more trees are felled for timber than to clear the land. Nearly all the hardwood – the solid wood with the beautiful grain that we use for furniture – comes from tropical rainforests.

One of the most important timbers for furniture is mahogany, which comes from South American forests and from similar species of trees that flourish in Africa. Teak, also used for furniture, comes from Burma, Thailand, India and some other parts of Southeast Asia. Iroko from Africa is often used in place of teak. After the Second World War the light-coloured timber, ramin, from Indonesia and Malaysia, was introduced to Europe and the United States and is used for furniture.

Greenheart from Guyana is known to all anglers because it is often used for fishing rods, but it is also used for lock-gates on canals. Two other familiar woods come from the tropical rainforests of South America – balsa, one of the lightest woods and

The power saw can cut down a huge rainforest tree in a few minutes.

Felling by axe, shown here in Sumatra, is a laborious task.

Illustrated below are some familiar household items made from tropical hardwood. How many can you find in your home?

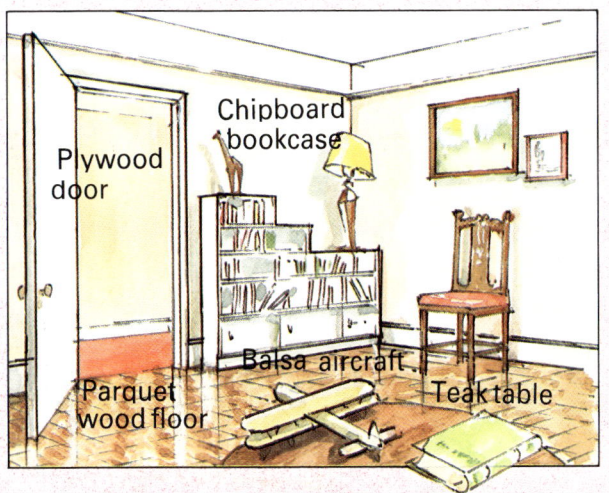

The main diagram below shows that hardwoods, most from tropical rainforests, form 21% of the world's timber. The small diagram shows that most of the hardwood comes from Third World countries of Africa, South America and Southeast Asia.

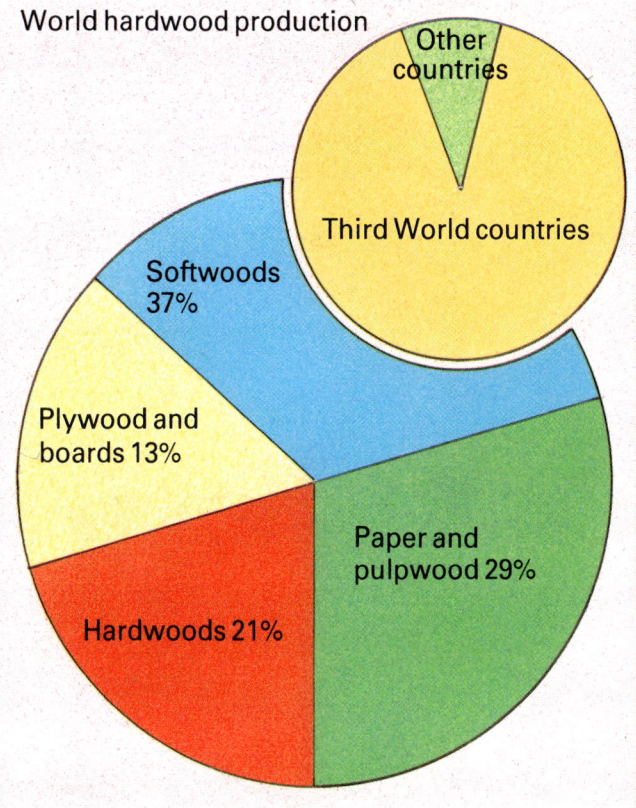

therefore much used by model aircraft builders, and brazilwood or pernambuco, formerly needed for dyeing and now used to make violin bows.

Japan, the USA, France and Britain are the main importers of tropical hardwood. Countries that harvest and sell the wood include Brazil, Burma, Colombia, Indonesia, Malaysia and Thailand.

A great deal of the timber is converted in Europe to plywood, blockboard, wood pulp and other products, which are then exported back to the countries where the trees grew. Indeed Nigeria, once a major timber exporter, imports far more in finished form than it sells as logs.

Because of the size of tropical trees and the difficulties of removing the logs, many loggers today use huge high-powered machines. Unfortunately, these damage surrounding trees, as well as those intended to be felled. From the conservationist's point of view, traditional hand-felling methods are preferable to modern chain saws and bulldozers.

A bulldozer clears the ground, following logging in the Indonesian rainforest.

Other rainforest products

The rainforests are a storehouse of many useful products, besides timber. One is rubber. Latex, the milky substance which contains rubber, occurs in about 1,800 trees and plants. The best comes from the Pará rubber tree which grows wild in the Amazon rainforest. It is now cultivated in Southeast Asia. Gutta-percha, a substance similar to rubber, comes from trees in the Malaysian rainforest, while sapodilla, which grows in Belize, Guatemala and Mexico, yields chicle, used to make chewing gum.

Many of our foods originated in tropical rainforests, including bananas, cacao (cocoa-beans), cashew nuts, cassava (the source of tapioca), coconuts, coffee, aubergines, guavas, lemons, oranges, papayas, peanuts, pineapples, potatoes and tea. A new sweetening agent may come from a plant that has recently been discovered in the rainforest of West Africa. It is said to be 3,000 times sweeter than sugar.

The forests are also the source of many vegetable oils, which are used for making foodstuffs, flavourings, perfumes, paints and soap. They include banana oil and palm oil.

One in four of the medicines in daily use has its origin in a plant that grew in the rainforests. An outstanding example is quinine, used to treat malaria. It comes from the bark of the chicona tree, which flourishes in the forests of Peru. Curare, a deadly poison used by the Amerindian hunters to kill their prey, yields drugs now used to relax tense muscles and to treat multiple sclerosis.

Chemists are now working on about 1,400 plants which may possibly yield drugs that can be used for treating cancer sufferers. The first to be tested were types of periwinkle from the rainforests of Madagascar and the West Indies.

The forests may also hold the answer to the feared shortage of petroleum that is forecast in the next fifty years. The sap of the copaiba tree, which grows in Brazil, has been found to be almost identical to diesel fuel.

A Brazilian girl extracts latex from a rubber tree.

Bananas are a valuable crop on the island of Martinique in the West Indies.

CHAPTER 6 RAINFORESTS IN DANGER

The importance of rainforests

The tropical jungles and rainforests are the world's oldest wild places. Scientists believe that some rainforests, notably that of Malaysia, have existed for at least 40,000,000 years. The size of each forest has varied with changes in the earth's climate, especially during the alternating ice ages and interglacial periods of the past 2,000,000 years.

Traces of former rainforests have been found in non-tropical regions, such as Britain and Alaska. The forests flourished when these places were much nearer the equator than they are today, before the continents drifted apart.

Because of their age, the rainforests form a unique and irreplaceable bank of genetic material. As plant breeders require new varieties, and as pharmacists seek new medicines, they will have to turn to the forests for their material.

It used to be thought that the forests were a major source of oxygen, but in fact they are in a state of equilibrium – that is, they consume as much oxygen as they produce. However, the forests have a considerable effect on local weather conditions. A forest acts like a sponge, holding the rainwater that falls on it. The roots take up water from the soil before it can drain away and pump it up the trunk to the leaves. A big tree takes in many hundreds of litres of water a day. About half this water is released back into the atmosphere through the leaves, to fall again as rain. Where forests have been cut down, the water runs away and the

The rainforest water cycle
The diagram on the left shows the importance of rainforests in the water cycle. Rainforest trees require a great deal of water for their growth. The huge trees absorb water from underground streams through their vast roots. Later they release it back into the atmosphere by their leaves, in the process called transpiration. The evaporated water condenses in the atmosphere to form clouds and falls again as rain. So the rainforest trees play a vital role in storing rainwater and releasing it back into the atmosphere. As more rainforest trees are cut down, this natural balance is upset. If most of the world's rainforest is lost, this may have a major effect upon the climate of rainforest regions, and perhaps the world as a whole.

Huge trees, like the silk cotton tree of the Amazon rainforest, play a major role in the water cycle.

rainfall diminishes.

Some scientists fear that if the destruction continues, the world's climate may be permanently altered. Forests absorb a great deal of carbon dioxide, and so help to keep under control the amount of this gas in the atmosphere. The burning of fossil fuels is already pumping excessive carbon dioxide into the air, and the huge forest fires that accompany logging or clearing add more.

As carbon dioxide builds up in the earth's atmosphere it traps the sun's heat, just like the glass of a greenhouse. This 'greenhouse effect' warms up the surface of the earth, and in time it could melt the polar ice, raising the sea level and submerging low-lying coastal lands.

Deforestation and erosion

The diagram on the right shows erosion occurring in a rainforest area where many of the trees have been cleared. Extensive felling of rainforest trees will have serious long-term effects. When the trees are gone, rain can no longer be absorbed and so drains off the ground. Gradually the topsoil is washed away by the excess rainwater and the remaining soil becomes poor, losing its nutrients. The soil that has been washed away accumulates in the rivers, causing them to become blocked up with silt. When the tropical rainstorms occur, the silted-up rivers cannot absorb the heavy rain and burst their banks, causing extensive flooding. This has already happened in parts of South America where areas of rainforest are being cleared.

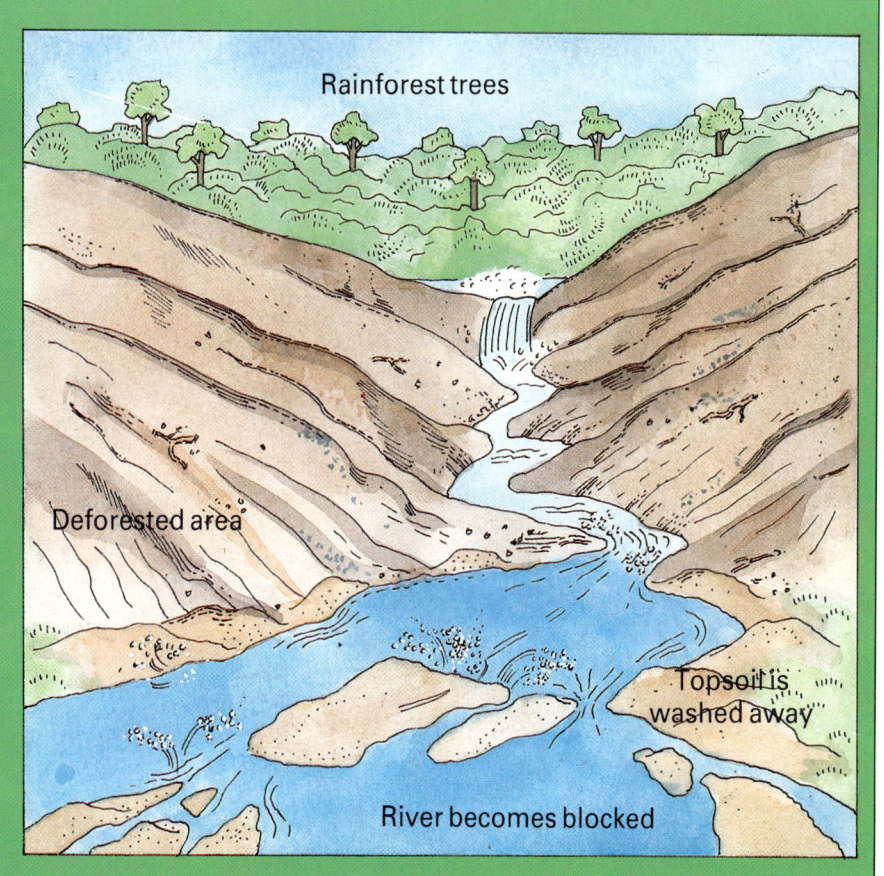

The disappearing rainforests

The world's rainforests are being destroyed at an ever-increasing rate. Since the end of the Second World War in 1945 over 40 per cent of the forests have been cut down. The rate of destruction has been estimated at 12 hectares (30 acres) a minute, day and night. For some countries the results will be catastrophic. For example, Nigeria and Panama will have no tropical forest at all by the year 2000 if felling continues at the present rate, while Costa Rica, Ecuador, Ghana, Ivory Coast and Thailand will retain a mere fraction of theirs.

Besides logging and farming, three things pose a major threat to the rainforests: mining, fire and water. Valuable mineral deposits often lie under the forests, and to extract them means completely removing the trees. The mining operation often leads to pollution of forest rivers. This has happened in Papua New Guinea.

Fire frequently follows logging as a way of clearing away the unprofitable brushwood left after the marketable timber has been hauled out. Such blazes can get out of control. One fire in Indonesian Borneo raged for ten months, destroying an area the size of Switzerland.

A consequence of deforestation is that the rainwater that would have been stored in the forests runs away, carrying the precious soil with it into the rivers. One tropical storm can sweep away 175 tonnes of soil from one hectare of land (70 tonnes an acre). Choked with eroded soil, the rivers flood, causing widespread damage and loss of life.

The building of dams for hydroelectric schemes also destroys large areas of forest. The Itaipu Dam on the Paraná River between Brazil and Paraguay has flooded an area about the size of Greater London, while the construction of the new Tucururi Dam on the Tocatins River in Brazil will cause the loss of six American Indian towns.

The rapidly expanding tourist industry in, for example, New Guinea, Ivory Coast and Queensland, Australia, also poses a threat to the future of rainforests.

Construction of an iron ore mine in Southern Pará State, Brazil.

This road cuts through remote rainforest in Central Africa, where Pygmies have lived undisturbed for thousands of years.

This graph shows the estimated rainforest loss by the year 2000.

How much rainforest have we lost?

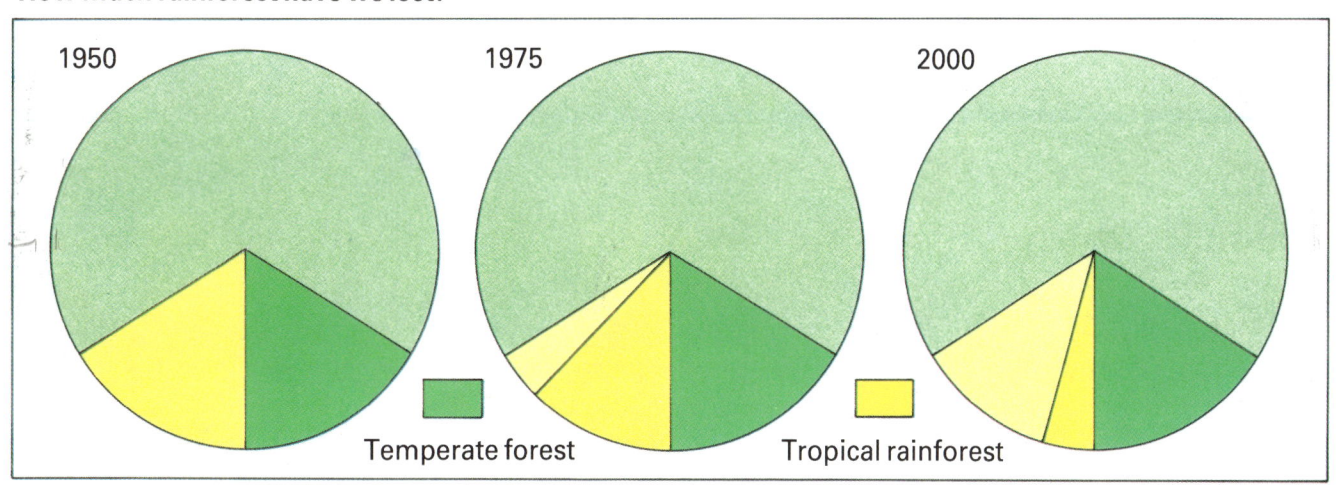

The three pie charts above compare the loss of rainforest with that of temperate forest. In 1950 equal amounts of rainforest and temperate forest covered 30% of the world's land area. Temperate forests still cover the same area of land as in 1950, and are likely to in future, because they are maintained by reforestation. The world's rainforest, however, had already decreased by 20% in 1975, and by the year 2000 well over 50% of our rainforest could have disappeared unless steps are taken to reduce the rate of destruction.

39

The threat to wildlife and people

The damage to the landscape that follows extensive clearance of rainforest is obvious. Less obvious is the equally severe damage to animals and humans. Already a number of the animal species we know are in danger, including the orang-utan of Borneo, the eight species of Asian tigers, the Sumatran rhinoceros, the Malaysian tapir, the Malaysian elephant, the lemurs of Madagascar and their relation, the aye-aye. Moreover, many species may die out before they are even classified.

Forest peoples are also in danger. For example, before Europeans arrived in South America about 4,000,000 Amerindians lived in the Amazon region. Today fewer than 100,000 survive. The Brazilian government has promised to protect the Indians and their culture, but it is also opening up the Amazon region, which automatically puts the Indians' way of life in danger. The forest dwellers of Africa face similar problems.

In Indonesia the government has moved 3,600,000 people from the overcrowded islands of Bali, Java and Madura to Irian Jaya, the Indonesian half of New Guinea. As a result thousands of the original inhabitants have fled eastwards to Papua New Guinea. Another 65,000,000 people are scheduled to move to Irian Jaya.

The simultaneous problems of flooding and water shortage resulting from forest clearance are likely to have much wider effects. The recent devastating Ethiopian famine was partly due to the destruction of half the country's forests and the consequent widespread erosion, rendering the soil useless for agriculture. Deforestation in the Indian subcontinent has caused water and soil to flow off bare hillsides, resulting in terrible floods in Bangladesh.

Meanwhile shortages of drinking water are beginning to affect cities like Kuala Lumpur in Malaysia and Bangkok in Thailand because the forests that retained the water no longer exist.

Black lemurs in the Madagascan rainforest.

People under threat

The traditional lifestyle of many rainforest peoples is becoming increasingly threatened. Many Amerindians of South America (right) and Pygmies of Central Africa (below) have had to leave their homes, so that the area can be cleared for farming or forestry. Those who remain may abandon their traditional lifestyle, as new settlers bring modern technology to the quiet forests. Rainforest peoples also risk catching diseases, introduced by the new settlers, such as measles, influenza and tuberculosis, against which they have no natural immunity.

Saving the rainforests

The reason for the widespread destruction of rainforests is an economic one. The forests lie in underdeveloped countries which badly need to sell their timber in order to earn foreign currency. But present ways of logging are wasteful. Only the best timber from a few species is taken. In the logging process, other valuable trees are damaged and wood that is not wanted is burned. Hand-felling methods, while less profitable, do less damage. In Burmese forests elephants were traditionally used to move logs to the nearest river for floating downstream. Specially trained elephants may be used in future for logging in Asia, and this would certainly reduce damage to trees.

Some countries, such as Malaysia and Uganda, are already making use of wood that was previously wasted. Replanting of deforested areas as soon as the timber has been extracted helps to conserve the forests, and is already in progress in Gabon and Zambia. In replanting schemes suitable crop trees like oil palms or rubber trees are used. Terracing bare hillsides helps to retain water and so prevent the soil from being washed away. Such measures, however, can never replace the natural beauty of ancient rainforests. When a rainforest area is cleared, some unique species of tree are lost forever. Those species that can be regrown will take centuries to reach maturity.

At present the outlook for the rainforests is bleak, but people are realizing the very serious dangers of rainforest destruction. Conservation and environmental groups, such as the World Wildlife Fund and Friends of the Earth, are putting pressure on governments to control the destruction of rainforests and to protect their wildlife for the future. A number of countries have preserved areas of rainforest as national parks or nature reserves, so ensuring their future survival. So far, however, only four per cent of the forests are protected. The future of the rest, and of the animals that live in them, lies very much in our hands.

This young orang-utan is cared for in a special reserve in Sabah state, Malaysia.

Areas cleared of rainforest are often replanted with terraces of rubber trees which help prevent erosion.

Right Will rainforests survive into the next century?

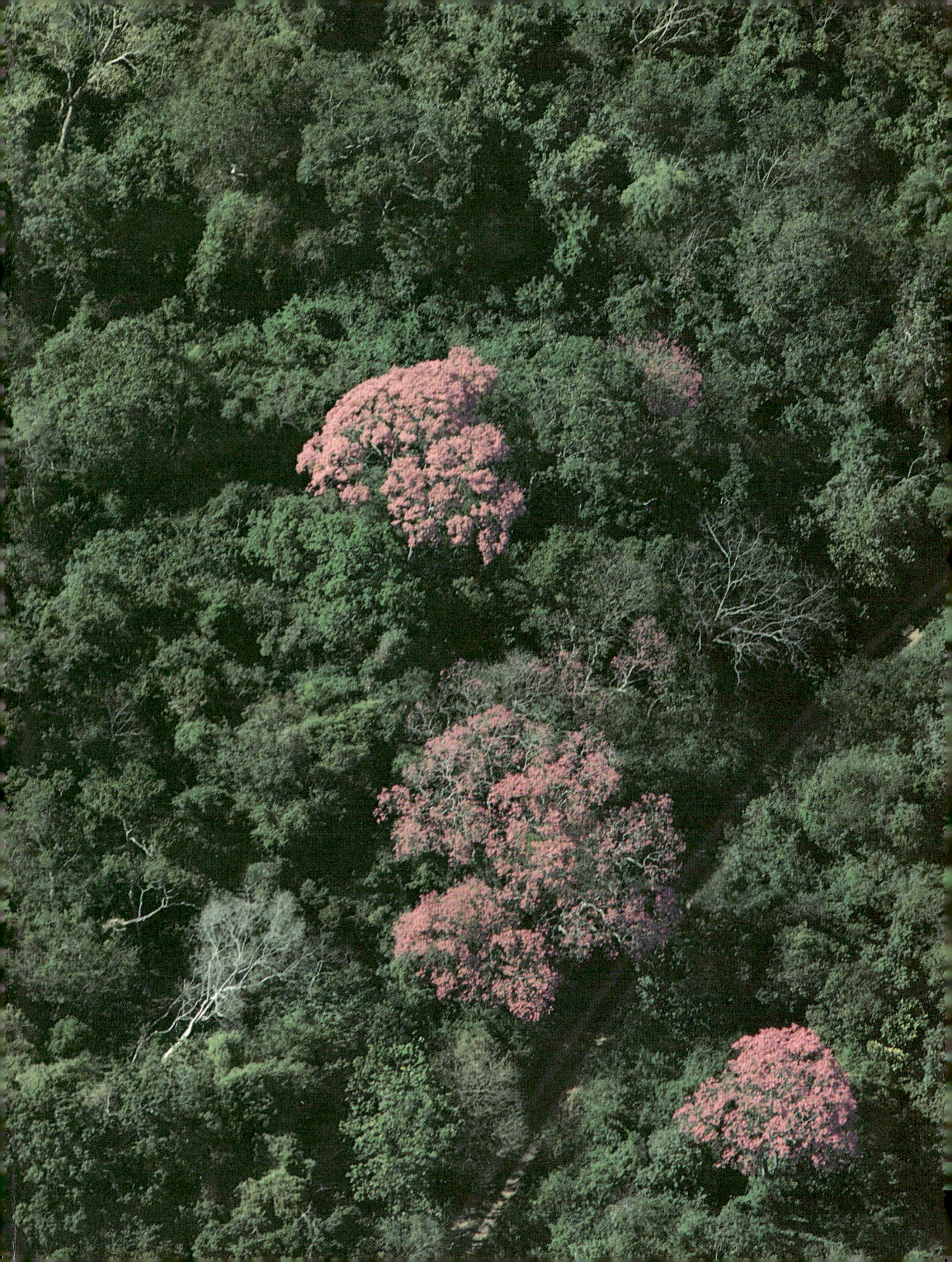

Glossary

Broadleaved evergreen A tree with wide leaves which it sheds a few at a time all the year round.
Bromeliad A plant of the pineapple family, mostly with the leaves forming a rosette; many grow on trees as epiphytes.
Buttress root A prop-like root which grows from the trunk of a rainforest tree and acts as a support.
Canopy The main umbrella-like top layer of a tropical rainforest, composed of the tree-tops.
Cash crops Crops grown for sale rather than for food.
Continental drift The movement of the continents across the surface of the earth.
Decomposers Organisms that break down dead vegetable or animal material into its component chemicals.
Deforestation The large-scale felling of trees for timber or for clearance purposes.
Ecosystem A group of living things which relate to one another and to their environment.
Emergent layer The scattering of very tall trees that emerge above the level of the canopy.
Epiphyte A plant that grows on another but does not take nourishment from it, as do parasites.
Erosion The wearing away of the earth's surface by the action of wind, water and weather.
Fossil fuels Naturally occurring fuels, such as coal and petroleum, formed by the decomposition of prehistoric organisms.
Gondwanaland The ancient southern continental landmass, supposed to have consisted of Antarctica, Africa, India, South America and Australia.
Greenhouse effect The retention of heat in the atmosphere by carbon dioxide and some other gases, which are increasing in the atmosphere as a result of pollution. The carbon dioxide allows the sun's rays through to the earth, but prevents them from escaping back into space, so warming the atmosphere, rather like a greenhouse retains heat.
Habitat The place where a plant or animal lives.
Hardwood The wood of a broadleaved tree; the wood itself may actually be soft, as in balsa.

Ice age Any period in time when much of the earth's surface is covered with ice.
Interglacial period A warmer period in the earth's history between ice ages.
Laurasia The ancient northern continental landmass, supposed to have consisted of North America, Europe and Asia.
Liana A woody climbing plant of tropical rainforests.
Mangrove A tropical evergreen tree which has downward-growing stiltlike roots and colonizes coastal land margins or inland swamps. The word mangrove also refers to the swampy habitat created by mangrove trees.
Marsupials A group of mammals whose young are born semi-developed and continue their growth in their mother's pouch, or marsupium.
Monotremes Egg-laying mammals of Australia and New Guinea.
Pangaea The ancient landmass that is thought to have split up into Gondwanaland and Laurasia.
Parasite A plant or animal which lives on another and takes nourishment from it.
Prehensile Adapted for grasping, by wrapping around a support.
Pygmies The hunter-gatherer peoples of Asia and Africa who are usually less than 1.5 m (5 ft) tall.
Saprophyte A plant or animal that obtains its nourishment from dead plants or animals.
Scavenger An animal that eats rotting flesh.
Species A classified group of plants or animals.
Transpiration The natural loss of water into the air which occurs in leaves.
Tropics The part of the earth's surface between the tropics of Cancer and Capricorn.
Understorey The layer of lower trees beneath the canopy of tall rainforest trees.
Vine A plant with a long, supple stem that creeps along the ground or climbs up a tree, clinging on with tendrils.

Further reading

David Attenborough, *The Living Planet* (Collins BBC, 1984)
Mary Batten, *The Tropical Forest Ants, Animals and Plants* (Faber and Faber, 1972)
Catherine Caufield, *In the Rainforest* (Heinemann, 1985)
S. Dillon-Ripley, *The Land and Wildlife of Tropical Asia* (Time-Life, 1965)
Violet Graham, *The Ecology of Rainforests* (Franklin Watts, 1975)
Robin Hanbury-Tenison, *Mulu: The rainforest* (Weidenfeld and Nicolson, 1980)
Schuyler Jones, *Pygmies of Central Africa* (Wayland, 1985)
Andrew Langley, *Timber* (Wayland, 1986)
Gillian Morgan, *Jungles and People* (Wayland, 1982)
Marion Morrison, *Indians of the Amazon* (Wayland, 1985)
François Nectoux, *Timber* (Friends of the Earth, 1985)
Charles Secrett, *Rainforest* (Friends of the Earth, 1985)

Picture acknowledgements

The publishers would like to thank the following for allowing their photographs to be reproduced in this book: Bruce Coleman Limited *front cover* main picture (Eric Crichton), *back cover* (WWF/Paul Wachtel), 7 below (Dieter and Mary Plage), 11 (Frans Lanting), 12 (Eric Crichton), 14 left (Michael Fogden), 14 right (Leonard Lee Rue), 16 above (Michael Fogden), 16 below (L C Marigo), 19 below (Alain Compost), 22 (H Rivarola), 24 right (Simon Trevor), 25 (H Rivarola), 29 (C B Frith), 30 (Dieter and Mary Plage), 32 below (Mike Price), 38 (L C Marigo), 40 (Vincent Serventy); Geoscience Features Picture Library 6, 13 above, 19 above and 22 below (M D Hirons); Hutchison Library 5, 39, 41 below (Sarah Errington); Marion and Tony Morrison 7 above, 13 below, 37, 43; Tun Abdul Razak Laboratory 42 below; ZEFA 17 (E & P Bauer), 20 (R Halin), 21 above, 23 above (Horus), 23 below, 24 left (R Halin), 27 (G H Lee), 32 above (Bramaz) 35 (K Kerth), 41 above (H Halin), *front cover* inset picture (A Roberts). All the illustrations are by Elsa Godfrey.

Index

Aerial roots 13, 20
Africa 8, 14, 16, 18, 26, 28, 30, 32, 33, 34, 36
Alaska 36
Amazon rainforest 8, 14, 19, 24, 26, 28, 34, 40
Amazon River 6, 8
Amerindians 26, 28, 40
Andes 8, 28
Animals 4, 14, 16, 23, 40
Antarctica 18
Ants 16, 24
Asia 14, 16, 22, 26
Australasia 8, 14
Australia 6, 8, 18, 20, 21, 22, 23, 38
Aye-aye 40

Bali 40
Beef cattle 30
Beetles 16
Belize 34
Benin 8
Biami tribe 26
Birds 14, 23
Birds of paradise 23
Borneo 18, 26, 38
Bowerbirds 23
Brazil 8, 34, 40
Britain 33, 36
Bromeliads 19
Burma 8, 32
Bushmen 26
Butterflies 13, 14, 24
Buttress roots 4

Camouflage 24
Canopy 4, 10, 12, 14, 20, 24
Cassowaries 23
Central America 6, 30
Chewing gum 34
China 6, 8

Climate 6, 8, 36
Cloud forests 6, 20
Cobaea scandens 13
Cock-of-the-rock 16
Cockroaches 16
Colombia 8
Columbus, Christopher 28
Conquistadores 28
Conservation 42
Continental drift 18, 36
Costa Rica 38
Crabs 20
Crops 30

Decomposers 16
Deforestation,
 consequences of 36, 38, 40, 42

Echidna 22
Ecuador 8, 38
Elephants 16, 40
Emergent layer 10, 12
Endangered species 40
Epiphytes 12–13, 19
Equator 4, 6, 8, 36
Erosion 36, 38
Ethiopia 40
Europe 4, 32
Explorers 28

Famine 40
Farming 30–31
Ferns 20
Flooding 40
Flowers 10–11, 18–19
Flying fox 14
Forest fires 36, 38
France 33
Friends of the Earth 42
Fruit bats 14
Fungi 11, 16

Gabon 42
Ghana 8, 38
Gibusi tribe 26
Goliath beetle 24
Gondwanaland 18, 22
Greenhouse effect 36
Guatamala 34
Guianas, the 8
Guinea 8
Guyana 32

Honey badger 23
Humboldt, Baron von 28
Hummingbirds 13, 23
Hydroelectricity 38

Ice ages 36
India 16, 18, 23, 32
Indicator bird 23
Indonesia 8, 19, 32, 40
Insects 24–5
Interglacial periods 36
Ipomoeas 13
Irian Jaya 40
Itaipu dam 38
Ivory Coast 38

Jaguar 16
Japan 33
Java 40
Jungle 4, 10, 16, 24, 30
Jungle cat 16
Jungle fowl 16

Kalahari desert 26

Laurasia 18, 22
Lemurs 23, 40
Leopard 16
Lianas 10
Liverworts 10

Livingstone, David 28
Lizards 14
Logging 8, 33, 36, 42
Lorises 23

Madagascar 8, 23, 34
Madura 40
Malay Peninsula 8, 40
Malaysia 8, 16, 30, 32, 34, 36, 42
Mangroves 6, 20
Marsupials 14, 22
Mbuti tribe 26
Medicines 34
Mexico 8, 34
Millipedes 16
Mining 38
Monkeys 14, 20, 22
Monotremes 22
Monsoon 6
Monsoon forests 6, 20
Montane forests 6, 20
Morpho butterfly 24
Mosses 10, 20
Mouse deer 16
Mudskippers 20

Napo River 28
National parks 42
Nature reserves 42
New Guinea 8, 14, 20, 21, 22, 23, 27, 36, 40
New Zealand 8, 20
Niger River 28
Nigeria 8, 33, 38
North America 4

Ocelot 16
Orang-utan 40
Orchids 13
Orellana, Francisco de 28
Oxygen 36

Pacific islands 8
Panama 38
Pangaea 18
Paraguay river 8
Paraná river 8, 38
Park, Mungo 28
Parrots 14
Passion flower 13
Peru 34
Phalangers 13
Pheasants 16
Philippines 8, 27, 30
Pizarro, Gonzalo 28
Plants, diversity of 4, 18
Platypus 20
Pollination 12–13
Population, increase in 30
Possums 14
Praying mantis 24
Pygmies 26

Quetzals 23
Quinine 34

Rafflesia 19
Rainfall 12, 36
Rainforests
 age of 4, 36
 classification of 6–7
 destruction of 36, 38, 40, 42
 distribution of 8–9
 effect on climate 36
 inhabitants 26–7, 40
 resources 34–5
Rainstorms 6
Replanting schemes 42
Rhinoceros, Sumatran 40
Robber-fly 24
Rondônia region, Brazil 31
Royal antelope 16
Rubber 34

Saprophytes 10
Shifting cultivation 30–31
Sianh Dyak tribes 26
Sloth 12, 24
Snakes 14, 16
South America 8, 13, 18, 19, 20, 22, 24, 26, 30, 32, 40
Southeast Asia 8, 16, 18, 20, 23, 27, 30, 32, 34
South Korea 8
Stanley, Henry Morton 28
Stick insects 24
Subtropical rainforests 6, 20
Sumatra 19
Sunbirds 23
Swallowtail butterfly 24

Tapir, Malaysian 40
 South American 16
Temperate zone 4
Temperature 12
Termites 16, 24
Thailand 8, 38, 40
Third World 30
Tiger 16, 40
Timber 32–3, 42
Tocatins river 38
Togo 8
Toucans 23
Tourism 38
Transpiration 20
Tree ferns 20
Tree frogs 14, 19
Tree kangaroos 14
Trees
 adaptations of 20
 conifers 20
 deciduous 20
 evergreen 4, 20
Tribes 26–7
Tropical fruits 12, 14, 34

Tropical hardwoods 32–3
Tropical rainforests 4, 6, 20
Tropics, the 4, 18
Tucururi dam 38

Uganda 42
Understorey 10
United States 30, 32, 33

Victoria amazonica 19
Vines 13
Vultures 16

Wallace, Alfred Russel 22
Water lily, giant 19
Water shortages 40
West Indies 8, 34
World Wildlife Fund 42
Worms 16

Zaïre 26
Zaïre river 8, 26, 28
Zambia 42